I0765848

Angela Langford Harrison

Why Worry ... 5 truths how you are sabotaging your happiness

Angela Langford Harrison

Angela Langford Harrison

1st Edition
copyright 2019 Why Worry
This publication may not be reproduced, copied or reprinted in whole or in part without the written permission of Why Worry LLC.
Scripture quotations are from the New International Version of the Bible.

Dedication

In honor of my mother, Julia Gordon Langford. She was beautiful inside and out. I never saw her worried and she doesn't have worries now that she is resting.

CONTENTS

FOREWORD

When I first met Angela, I knew it was something amazingly different about her calm spirit. She makes it well known to others who is the source of strength and author of her faith. With that being said it is to no surprise that she would share how she keeps her inner peace.

Angela is very transparent. When we met years ago, it was during very overwhelming circumstances. We did not allow those circumstances to steal our peace, define who we are, or steer us off our path. During that time, I have come to know a pleasant, calm, caring and passionate woman. Now I realize how she can have such a gracious approach and outlook on life. She has an outlook on life that truly blesses everyone around her. She is a woman who truly practices what she believes.

Angela's book, 'Why Worry' is a testament on how to process challenging times and situations that is vital with maintaining good mental health. I am honored to recommend Angela's book to you. With all the obstacles and challenges we face in this world I guarantee you will take away something from this book that will speak to your inner peace and psychological well-being.

Dr. Ann Marie Howard, PhD in Psychology

INTRODUCTION

The definition of worry
Merriam – Webster dictionary defines worry as a transitive verb: to assail with rough or aggressive attack or treatment (torment). As a noun: mental distress or agitation resulting from concern usually for something impending or anticipated (anxiety).

As I did some research about worry, I found some famous and anonymous people had express their thoughts on the subject. Here are some quotes:

Worry is the stomach's worst poison – Alfred Nobel

You can't work through worry and fear rationally because fear isn't rational! – Marianne Williamson

What is going to happen will happen, whether we worry or not. – Ana Monnar

The mind that is anxious about future events is miserable – Seneca

Warning, this book should not be used to clinically diagnose yourself. If you are beset with worry, anxiety, stress, mental restless, grief or depression, then seek clinical help. Your emotions can be in a fragile state and a mental health professional can provide care for your wellbeing.

MY STORY

After fourteen years of marriage, my husband decided to entertain the requested desires of a 21-year-old. Not a problem. We could go get counseling to help us cope with the early stage of his mid-life crisis. After one counseling session, it became apparent that counseling was not the answer. It would not fix anyone who felt that they did not need to be fixed. It would not fix anything. If a person believed that nothing was broken, would counseling help?

Seeking help or counseling can start you on a path of recovery. What you have just admitted to yourself was that you need assistance. You need a secondary party to look at your situation and to provide guidance. Someone who can give an unbiased opinion that only brings clarity. Not to add or take away but simplicity.

I didn't give myself a chance to continue with counseling. Although I was the only person participating, I should have continued the process. I became discouraged with the notion of it all myself after watching my therapist force himself to stay awake during one of our sessions. I did make a note to self: never make appointments right after lunch time. Carbohydrates tend to make oneself sleepy.

Well, there is nothing like being at a fork in the road and having a decision to make. And on top of that, several eyes are on you. Who is watching? Some family and friends are watching. One or two neighbors knew what was happening. Some friendly and some not so sympathetic.

I had to choose the path for me. My new friend/companion/confidant was worry. Not knowing if worry would let me down, embarrassed me or worst yet left me stranded. The only way I knew to make the pain, the depression and the worry stop was to hit rock bottom. At the bottom, no one came to check on me. I could tell people stood far away from me like I was the plague. What could they have been thinking? I don't want my marriage to end so I will stay away from her. I would still be undecided on which path to take. Choices, so many choices.

There I was left with so many tears that I could fill a jug. The panic episodes left me feeling deserted as I tried to care for three girls. This was the beginning or worry that turned into the "D" word – depression. Later in the book you will read about how I conquered worry to gain my happiness back.

IT IS A HABIT

Have you asked anyone; How are you doing? I am sure that you have. We use this greeting when we are being polite. We also use the phrase to inquire about someone's day. Think back to a time when your response to the question was, "Oh, I am well, just worried about" (then fill in the blank). Here is another one. "I am doing just great, but I am worried about" (again, fill in the blank). Often the fill in the blank response is kids, new job, health issues or even world events.

Now think back and recall the response. Did

the response always come from the same person? Now think again and recall if that repetitive response always come from you. Why is it that this response is always the same (fill in the blank)? Do you think a habit has been created? Is it too much of an effort to have a different response? One of the traits of worry is that we stick with the habit we have created. We create these routines of mindless responses and fixations.

Once we worry, for example on our health, we make it a habit of keeping the same response. We can't shake it because now it is in grained in us. It becomes a daily worry. Sometimes, we can be in a habit of mentioning health worries that it becomes second nature during conversations. Whenever people see you coming, we know you will have something to say about your knees.

If you have done the very best you can, worrying won't make it any better.

The rule of thumb is habits are created by repeatedly doing something for at least twenty-one days. If you find yourself doing the same thing day after day (excluding brushing your teeth), then I challenge you now to break your worry habit. Worry can be broken little by little, day by day. The parts of your thoughts should never equal the sum of your worry. Well what does that mean. Go one day with whatever is your issue, let's just say it is your health, not being on your mind. Replace it with a different response or action. Now, if part of your day was re-focused onto something else, then the sum of your day would not equal to worry.

I remember when I would get in the car, I would listen to gospel music for the first 30 minutes. This really helped me because I was in the habit of worrying as soon as I left my driveway. My mind would be all over the place until I had tears blinding my view. Only I knew how many times my life had been saved. Worrying about when my husband would come home consumed every minute of my day. Once, I was crying so intensely that I braked too hard which caused the car to swerve uncontrollably.

I nearly died from a car accident. I was consumed with thoughts of my marriage while driving to a group counseling session. This is when I had to veer off the rode to avoid striking a vehicle that suddenly stopped in front of me. A witness saw what happen and pulled fifty feet ahead in front of my car. He jogs back to where I was parked on the side of the road. He asked if I was alright. I responded yes. He then asked if he could pray with me. He said a prayer and I had thanked him for what he had done for me.

After this encounter with a stranger and several minutes on the side of the road, I realized I had to do something to save myself. I nearly died because I was more focused on could-of-would-of should-of thoughts. It finally registered with me that worrying had to stop. By shifting my thoughts onto something else, like singing along with the music, I was able to stop worrying during car rides.

◆ ◆ ◆

Angela Langford Harrison

20

DON'T MAKE IT A HABIT

Positive reinforcement always helps. Try invoking words of affirmation. Below are a few phrases:

I am love.

Joy is in my heart.

I will make the best of today.

When I smile, I feel as light as a feather.

Moving past all roadblocks today.

At this moment I am confident and enthusiastic.

I will only attract good energy.

How I feel on the inside will match how I look on the outside and vice versa.

First, choose a phrase or two. Next, take the phrase and post it where you can see it daily, preferably where your worry happens most often. For example, my worry would often happen first thing in the morning. I would have inspirational plaques hanging on the back of the bathroom door. My morning routine would also include a cup of coffee. I would have sticky notes on the cabinets. I would read them out loud to reinforce how I expected my day to be. This would also be a good time to involve a good friend or family member. Especially someone who expressed an interest in your wellbeing. An accountability partner can assist by:

*Mailing you a "thinking about you" card

*Choosing an odd hour to call to say hello

*Texting encouraging words just because it's Tuesday

◆ ◆ ◆

IT IS CONTAGIOUS

Have you given any thought as to how worry affects family, friends and loved ones? I am sure that you have not because I certainly did not. How could my pain be anyone else's pain? If I am worried about my marriage failing, that I am losing control of the situation and that I can't stop the embarrassment; than how does my pain affect my mother? It is because within our internal grief we pass symptoms like doubt and worry on to our family. We show loved ones how to act and or react to us.

Take my health for instance. Worrying about it passed on to my kids. My kids take those same thoughts and fears and passes them on to their friends or to their teachers. How does this happen? Well, if we see the cycle backwards, the teacher worries about my child not getting enough sleep at night, and my child worries that I don't get enough sleep at night and I don't get enough sleep at night because I am worrying about my failing health. So, my action has caused worry to be contagious when it really wasn't warranted.

Worry is no longer a thing that I can call my own. Because I have contaminated others, I have brought them to an unfortunate state. The only way to stop the effect of worry is to resolve my situation. Then once it has stopped, embarrassment is left behind. I worked to get my health under control. My child no longer sees my health as an urgent issue. Yet, the teacher asked me if my child is getting enough sleep over my perceived worry from 9 months ago. How embarrassing is that!

One day you'll look back and realize that you worried too much about things that really didn't matter.

Worry not only triggers anxiety and stress for you but for those in your circle as well. One of the best ways to defeat worry is to keep it to yourself. Really? Yes, really. I mean, daily worry should be your own thing because you birth it. You watered the seed. You attended to it when no one else would. I tell you that it is in your best interest to not share it as if passing out candy.

There is a difference between concern and worry. Learn the difference then practice what you have learned. It is important to know the difference for a health state of mind. One thought or even one day of worry doesn't destroy your world. You choose how and when you will conquer this unwelcomed and unnatural control of your mind. Our loved ones should be concerned for us, not inundated with worry because we made a situation contagious.

DON'T MAKE IT CONTAGIOUS

Take a closer look at your circle of influence. Your circle could be made up of people with who you spend most of your time. Your circle could be people with the same agenda as yours. Also, your circle could be a team that focuses on one goal. If you don't have a circle, then I am sure there is one person in your life that you can't see contaminating.

Look at the list below and decide who in your life you are affecting:

➢   A parent

- ➤ A child
- ➤ A best friend
- ➤ A mentor
- ➤ A co-worker

Have you ever arrived home from the grocery store to find that one of your oranges appears to have green fuzz on it? What do you do? Most would immediately throw out the moldy orange and separate the oranges with a thorough inspection. We would wash and dry each orange that could be saved and hope that the rest weren't contaminated.

How can we apply this same pattern to our thoughts? Let's try this, focus on that one person and decide how you will stop the contamination. If we chose the co-worker, then we can decide not to have conversations that include worry. I am choosing not to talk about my marriage and the lack of sleep that I am getting. My co-worker then has no reason to worry about my lack of sleep. They no longer have a worry that needed to be shared with the supervisor. My Supervisor then has no worries that I can't continue to be a productive employee due to sleep deprivation. The owner of the company doesn't have to worry about an imaginary accident on the job that will involve OSHA.

Catch thoughts of worry immediately. Throw it out of the conversation and replace it with something else. As a child, I learned from my grandmother that you can never go wrong talking about the weather. As an adult, I have learned to give compliments as part of the conversation. You will soon learn that you can have meaningful conversations that doesn't cause worry or sound an alarm for others.

◆ ◆ ◆

IT IS ADDICTIVE

Have you ever watched a marathon of your favorite TV show? Have you eaten a half gallon of chocolate chip ice cream in one sitting? Have you participated in an aerobics class twice a day for fourteen days straight? These examples are what I call temporary addictions. I watched season one of House of Cards straight through. My mind was always fixated on what was going to happen next. I immediately needed to know how things would end.

When your mind is fixated on something long term, then that is a mental addiction. In my situation, I would wake up worrying, I would run errands and be worrying. I could be waiting for the waiter to return with a glass of water and worry the entire three minutes. I just didn't feel right if I was not worrying about something. And in my case, it was my marriage. It became something I just had to do. One time I got forty-five minutes of sleep for the entire night. I just could not turn my mind off when I went to sleep for the night.

Stop worrying about what can go wrong and get excited about what can go right.

When worrying becomes part of your daily routine, like taking a shower, then it is an addiction that must be treated. Seeking professional help is imperative. And when you are not worrying, you think something is wrong with you. Why is that? Because worrying starts to be a good thing. It starts to feel good. Imagine that its winter. Worry is your soft, warm blanket. In a strange way, worrying turns into normalcy. Worry becomes so normal that you will internally welcome it. Worry can be expected as a reoccurring action that must be performed.

Being on pins and needles should not result in good feelings. An unhealthy worry starts to separate you from family and friends. The separation that occurs is exactly what one of the by-products of addiction is designed to do. It is A comfy feeling. You would rather be in the house worrying about your finances than to be at the park with your kids. Even to step outside the house to feel the warmth of the sun isn't enough. You would rather be isolated, enjoying the feeling of being at the kitchen table figuring out today how you are going to pay a bill that is due in 12 months.

◆ ◆ ◆

DON'T MAKE IT ADDICTIVE

There is nothing wrong with having an organized or scheduled life. In fact, it is the preferred method for me to use. Being organized leaves little room for daydreaming. The mind does not get a chance to wander because you are busy. Every block of time is account for by design. I often tell people I love having a full plate.

The chances of sitting in front of the TV are slim. No time for thinking about the past or about things that might occur in an imagined future. No opportunities to sit around worrying about what the future is going to look like because you are busy. So how do you get busy? Start with unwinding the mind. Below is a list of ways to get you started. Unwind the mind by:

➤ Reading for 15 to 30 minutes – plan it during a segment of your day. For example, choose morning before eating breakfast; noon after having lunch or evening before the nightly news.

➤ Completing a word puzzle – another great activity. You can find them in most dollar stores. There are websites which you can print them for free. Also, there are options on your smart phone. The physical puzzles are inexpensive and small; which can be carried in your purse or book bag. They can be placed in several areas such as night-stand or your office at work.

➤ Doing Yoga – this activity requires concen-tration. You will have to maintain your balance and focus. Worrying is not part of the equation. If you are a beginner, then learning poses, stretching and practicing is something that you will be doing often. Requirements are that you be able to hold your breath for 5-8 seconds. I know that I cannot hold my breath and worry about my high blood pressure at the same time.

IT IS A DEAL BREAKER

Have you heard the saying, No one likes a worry wort? Have you planned a birthday party then started to think about who would or wouldn't show up? Not only did you make a list of names, but you checked it twice and three times over. You checked it so often that you began to worry that those who said would come may not attend. Fear took over and you wait for the phone to ring. Overly concerned that the photographer and caterer would back out at the last minute. Your worry became so frequent that you rationalized no one would come so you cancelled the entire event.

This type of worry was the deal breaker for a party that was planned six months in advance. The time and money spent on the party, not to mention if other people were involved, was all for nothing. You worried so that you lost a night's sleep or two. The party was planned, and commitments were made. Therefore, whatever the outcome, we should be happy. Instead, worry checked in and you checked out. People get sick and cars break down. Emergencies happen to the best of us. All the fervent planning in the world can't stop some things from happening. Don't worry about things that you can't control.

Worrying is using your imagination to create something you don't want.

Worry can be the deal breaker in a lot of things; job, home life, community. Relationships are most often affected. During a new budding romance, there isn't much emphasis placed on finances. But once things become serious or an engagement happens, then we don't want to talk about finances. We will make excuse for our partners frugal ways or extravagant spending.

So, we turn to worry. Now we worry that the relationship will not last or worse, the engagement gets called off. Now your reaction over how your partner stewards their money is a deal breaker. Not once has a meaningful conversation about finances has been had. There could very well be a plausible explanation how money is managed. There could also be a justified reason why a budget is not used.

Worry keeps you stuck and unable to move forward. Imagine repeating how a situation will play out breaks the deal. In other words, worry becomes the icing on the cake and therefore we don't want a slice.

DON'T MAKE IT BE

A DEAL BREAKER

Remove worry - create an action plan by:

➤ Changing your attitude – Let's go back to the romance scenario for a minute. What if you stopped worrying to have the conversation about finances? You may realize that your partner frugal ways were only temporary. Maybe they were being an example of how to be responsible in some areas because he or she saw that you were extravagant in other areas. And, what about that slice of cake? If you could scrape the icing off would you still not want to eat it?

➤   Taking baby steps - Let's go back to the party scenario for a minute. Planning a party six months in advance can be a long way off. Most birthday parties do not require that much time. If you are overwhelmed or have little to no assistance, planning in stages would be a solution. During the first month you could create a theme. And the second month you could find a location. The third and fourth month you can secure any vendors and create menu/gift bags etc., The fifth month send out invites and sixth month send out reminders or confirmation e-mails.   It is easy to see how the mind has time to create problems where there are none. Worrying will be this deal breaker if you have 5 months of waiting to go through.

➤   Making time to meditate – Worry can't stop anything from happening when your pause doesn't allow it. What does that mean? Meditation creates an atmosphere where the mind gets to relax. For me, the best times are when I sit outside on my porch and focus on the birds chirping. I close my eyes and think about how natures sounds are very soothing and relaxing. I watch the squirrel's run and jump from tree to tree. It is imperative that we make time to give the mind a break from the thoughts that cause anxiety and nervousness. When you act to change your attitude, take baby steps or make time to meditate, you will find that worry doesn't have much of a home with you. Worry can't set up a shop in your mind. If you want happiness, then one way is to create an action plan.

◆ ◆ ◆

IT IS A SIN

Have you ever doubted that God would provide for all your needs? If so, then doubt is kin to worry and worry is a sin. Worry is your mind racing with fear and disbelief that your issue or situation will never be resolved. Having a mind of worry tells God that he is not big enough to handle your concern. If I have a worry big enough to take over some aspects of my life, then I really don't believe in a higher power.

Remember, worry is your imagination creating something that you don't want. Again, why would God give your mind something that you don't need. "Worry implies that we don't trust God is big enough, powerful enough or loving enough to take care of what's happening in our lives." – Francis Chan. As for me, I no longer worry about being abandoned, embarrassed or not being in control. I gave all worry to God to let Him deal with it. As my father, he has far more experience than I do. He is caring and protects those who are left with no resources. The community watches but God is of action. Who was I to try to handle it all when He sits on high?

Do not be anxious about anything but in every situation by prayer and petition, with thanksgiving, present your request to God. And the peace of God, which transcends all understanding, will guard your hearts and your minds in Christ Jesus. NIV Phil 4:6-7

Once I understood that my worrying was an offence to God, I stopped. The feeling in my legs returned. I started back eating regularly. No longer did I need to attend group counseling sessions for depression. When I let things take its course, my life became constant and clear. As awful as the demise of my marriage was, not having to worry was the best thing that happen to me.

Now this was a situation for God to work wonders. This worry/problem regarding my marriage had to happen so that God could get the glory. I had to go through it to share with you and others. It was all part of God's plan. I stood on faith while not knowing tomorrows outcome because I just couldn't worry about that anymore. My breakthrough was understanding that to worry was calling The Lord a liar. How could I believe that He is my provider (Genesis 22:13-14) and my peace (Judges 6:24) yet I continued to worry over my future. I immediately snapped out of my funk. Worrying was not true to my fundamental belief. I choose happiness. I can share my story with others freely now because I am happy.

Angela Langford Harrison

DON'T MAKE

IT A SIN

When you are mired in worry, it will shake the strongest of faiths. Plan to set aside additional study time in the Bible.

Below are a few scriptures that you can assign to a day of the week for enhanced devotional.

➢ For a word on Study

Ezra 7:10

Psalm 119:15

Luke 12:26

➢ For a word on Peace

John 14:27 1

Peter 5:7 John 16:33

2 Thessalonians 3:16

➢ For a word on Worry

Philippians 4:6

Matthew 6:25

➢ For a word on Faith

Ephesians 2:8

Hebrews 11:1

Mathew 21:21

◆ ◆ ◆

CONCLUSION

Have I shared enough truths with you? Can you see just how the act of worrying sabotages your happiness? Worry is not about always being concerned about a problem. Worry can be a part of situations that just doesn't get any better. I have mentioned the fact that it is a control issue that you control.

• Worry is a habit that becomes a perpetual wheel. Can you imagine yourself a hamster? Worry is the hamster that goes on and on, non-stop. Imagine running on a wheel that goes to a place which doesn't exist.

• 	Worry is contagious to the point that it affects family and friends. If you let it, just like a cold, the symptoms are there, but nothing is done to prevent the virus from spreading. It is up to you to wash your hands repeatedly. Often, we cover our cough and isolate our self to keep from infecting others. Use caution; don't isolate yourself from receiving help. The steps we do take are to not risk contaminating others.

• Worry can be addictive to the point that it feels good or brings some form of meaning to our life. If you drink a cup coffee, you may take it with a teaspoon or two of sugar and cream. Normally, we have it in the morning and sometimes with dinner. Now can you see yourself drinking 8-10 cups of coffee throughout the day with 4 tablespoons of sugar. Worrying, like the excessive cups of coffee, should not become addictive. It should not be something we do from the time we wake up until we go to sleep.

- Worry is the deal breaker that keeps us at home plate. No matter how much we practice, hitting the ball, we never hit a home run. When it is game time, we always foul out. We never advance because we have made worrying be the deal breaker to our plans in life. We must make plans in life that are important enough to see them through.

- Worrying is a sin. We all fall short of the glory of God. So, with worry we pray as to present our worry to God. Turning it over to Him to handle. Worry can be trouble for tomorrow and tomorrow is not promised to no man. There is no reasonable explanation as to why we worry when we don't have tomorrow. I tell you, go about today which the Lord has given in all its abundance to enjoy. You are special to Him. He gives new mercies every day in which we can relish in while he takes care of our worries.

Angela Langford Harrison

52

PARTING THOUGHTS

Sing-along with me
In every life we have some trouble
But when you worry you make it double
Don't worry, be happy
Don't worry, be happy now
(from the song "Don't Worry be Happy" by Robert McFerrin Jr.)

By Frank Outlaw
Watch your thoughts, they become your words;
Watch your words, they become your actions;
Watch your actions, they become your habits;
Watch your habits, they become your character;
Watch your character, they become your destiny.

ACKNOWLEDGEMENTS

Rev. Dr. Steven N. Dial Sr., Senior Pastor of Rainbow Park Baptist Church Decatur, GA (Thanks for your guidance)

Patricia, Sandra and Christine (Thanks for checking on me during this process)

Carlissa, Alexia and Celah (Thanks for always reminding me I had somewhere to be)

CONNECT WITH ME...

Facebook   Why Worry 411
Instagram   Whyworry411
Twitter   Why Worry LLC
WWW   whyworry.onuniverse.com
E-mail   whyworry411@yahoo.com

CONNECT WITH OTHERS...

Use the hashtags

\#whyworrythebook

\#whyworry411

\#happinessisthegoal

◆ ◆ ◆

...IT'S A MOVEMENT

- Mental Health
- Financial Wellness (coming soon)
- Retirement (spring 2020)

ABOUT THE AUTHOR

Angela Langford Harrison is the owner of Angie's Elegant Events and the founder of Why Worry LLC. She holds a Bachelor of Science degree in Business Administration from Mississippi University for Women. Also, Angela is a federal employee with 22 years of service.

Angela acknowledges her Lord and savior Jesus the Christ. She attributes her passion and purpose to God's word as written in the Holy Bible. The scripture that impacts her life the most is Jeremiah 29:11. She is a member of Rainbow Park Baptist Church in Decatur, GA where she is also a ministry leader.

Angela is originally from Columbus, Mississippi and currently resides in Atlanta, Georgia. She has 3 adult children and 2 grandchildren.

www.ingramcontent.com/pod-product-compliance
Lightning Source LLC
Chambersburg PA
CBHW051416250726
48655CB00003B/1080